THE JOB SEARCH PLAYBOOK

A Leader's Guide to Accessing the
Hidden Job Market

Andrew MacAskill

Copyright © 2021 by Andrew MacAskill.

All rights reserved. This book is protected by copyright. No part of this book may be reproduced or transmitted in any form or by any means, including as photocopies or scanned-in or other electronic copies, or utilized by any information storage and retrieval system without written permission from the copyright owner.

Printed in the United States of America.

Cover Design by 100Covers.com
Interior Design by FormattedBooks.com

Contents

Chapter 1: The Jumping Off Point: My Story 1

Chapter 2: The Challenges Of Modern Job Searching 7

Chapter 3: A Transformative Mindset Update 13

Chapter 4: Understanding What You Want 19

Chapter 5: The Go-To-Market Plan 25

Chapter 6: Generating Job Opportunities Through Your Network 35

Chapter 7: Generating Job Opportunities Online 41

Chapter 8: Getting Fit For Interviews 53

Chapter 9: Interview Performance 63

Chapter 10: Final Stage Presentations 71

Chapter 11: Offer Management and Salary Negotiation 79

Chapter 12: The First Ninety Days 85

CHAPTER 1

The Jumping Off Point: My Story

I'll never forget the day the text came through. It was 2.12pm on Monday 14th January 2019, when one of the two business owners I worked for sent it: "Can you meet me at the hotel at 3pm?"

I instantly knew what it meant, and I shook when I read the message. In my five years as Managing Director of their company, we had been on one heck of a rollercoaster ride, but I had never been summoned off-site, and even more significant was that it was the day before our 2019 kick-off meeting.

The previous six months had been tough and had damaged our numbers, so I realised this was the end. I had a spare fifty minutes before the meeting and thought it would be a good idea to update my wife, who was employed by the company as the Group Financial Controller. I asked her and our Operations Director to come into my office and explained I had been called off-site for a meeting, and I thought it safe to assume that I was being made redundant or there was going to be a significant change within the company.

As I walked over to the hotel, I started thinking about the team: There was the guy from the Midlands who had only just joined us and had a six-week-old baby and was due down early in the morning. There was the mum who had returned to work after ten years and who had experienced a new sense of confidence, and the guy whom I had convinced to join our mission just four months earlier. I felt responsible about the degree that it would affect their lives on my watch.

And then, of course, closer to home, was my wife, who had already suffered burn-out from the workload and drama of running the business alongside raising our young family. How would she deal with all the change that was to come? This was going to be testing.

Amid my whirring thoughts, my intuition nudged me to change my LinkedIn log in so that I would at least maintain control over my online following, which I had worked so hard to grow and nurture. I tried to compose myself as I walked and consciously advised myself to take care not to get angry or overly emotional in the meeting, whatever the outcome may be. I reminded myself of how it important it is to stay calm and true to your values even in volatile situations, and I repeated a favourite saying over and over in my head, that had served me well in the past: "Andrew, act as though your son is in the room with you."

Then I took a deep breath and entered the hotel bar, ready to face the firing squad. I couldn't see my boss, so I texted to let her know I had arrived, and she soon came through to join me. She had reserved a private room and was visibly nervous. She could be tough and occasionally even brusque, but she was someone I had grown incredibly close to over the years. As we developed the business, she kept us on track and pragmatically managed the differences of opinion between her husband, who was the Group CEO, and me. They had referred to me publicly as "like family", several times, and I cared for her deeply.

The bottom line was that it had all become too much for all of us to handle. I asked if she was okay and she told me she wasn't and that they had to shut the business down. They were closing the office and making me, my wife and our entire team redundant.

Shell-shocked, I managed to stay calm, and I said that I understood and offered my support for the inevitable challenges that were bound to arise. Then I left in a daze, clutching a small white envelope. They called my wife in next.

Once I got over the immediate shock, a feeling of immense relief coursed through me because the role had taken an incredible toll on my wellbeing and that of my family. Still, I had stubbornly refused to fall on my sword out of a sense of loyalty and my commitment to turn the company around despite the dysfunction and frequently challenging internal culture. I experienced a sense of guilt about my relief, knowing that lives would be affected and worrying that in the last six months I had not performed at the same level as in the previous four years. This internal flip-flop between relief and guilt had me in its grip for several days.

And so, in search of relief from my stressful thoughts, I did what many British men would do; I went to the pub and ordered a pint. The pub was our work local, where we had celebrated as a team, said goodbye to colleagues and enjoyed summer lunches in the sunshine. I sat nursing my pint, questioning what it had all been for…

Five years: five years of grinding, innovating, motivating, selling, negotiating, pushing, pulling, planning, reacting, fighting and supporting. And just like that, it was all over.

I had reviewed every proposal, won every pitch, interviewed every recruit, shown up on social media every day beating the drum and taking our mission to market and even had my brother-in-law decorate the office, printing our values and mission all over the walls.

The mission was aborted with the passing of an envelope. The business had been like an extension of me and such a key part of my identity that my mood seemed directly linked to its level of success.

My wife arrived at the pub in shock. She couldn't believe it was over. We were both emotional; my wife was anxious about the future, and I was full of regret for what could have been.

We couldn't understand why they hadn't told us before so that we could have prepared. Why were they doing this when the team was so strong? And most confusing: why did it hurt so much when deep down we didn't even want to be there anymore?

Ironically and luckily, three months before this day that turned my life around, I had set up an online career coaching business called *Executive Career Jump* and my employers, these same business owners, had backed it with cash for a shareholding. The new enterprise or 'side hustle' was very much my passion project as I loved using my fifteen years executive search experience to help out-of-work leaders to perform at their best and attract their next role.

As reality set in, I knew it was critical I do everything in my power to regain full ownership of Executive Career Jump as part of the settlement. I couldn't face another loss of something I loved, and the company was crucial for my family's future, but I feared that the stress of the sudden change had blurred my sharp commercial mind.

After a subdued journey home, my wife and I steeled ourselves to open our small white envelopes. I assumed I would get one month's notice in lieu, five weeks' full pay (one for every year) and perhaps some cash for the shares I held in their company. This would have allowed us some breathing room, and we would have been financially stable, but unfortunately, this was not to on offer. The content of my wife's envelope was equally underwhelming.

There was only a statutory five hundred pounds per week, per year, a request to work all of my notice and to transfer my shares back without compensation.

I was gutted, and my knee-jerk reaction was to fire off a couple of messages to two Recruitment leaders who had offered me employment opportunities in the past. My confidence had taken a severe knock, and I felt an urgent need to establish that I was still in demand. I received positive responses from them both, but I noticed that this desire for reassurance only gave me a quick boost of gratification. Later, after working with many more leaders who found themselves in similar situations, I realised external circumstances can't permanently fix feelings of insecurity because confidence comes from within us and depends purely on our state of mind in the moment.

I met with our former Operations Director at the local pub to try and console him. He was one in a million but prone to worry, so I wanted to reassure him he was qualified, powerful, and would come through this. He was exhausted after having worked until the early hours all weekend to prepare for the kick-off meeting that never came. We did our best to support each other and continue to do so, and I will always be grateful for his friendship and camaraderie during that stressful period.

When I returned home, I reread the letter and noticed that an email had gone out to the team advising of the change of plan. There was no strategy and kick-off meeting, but there would be a schedule of personal appointments. I longed to reach out to the team but had promised the owners I would wait, but I imagined the tough conversations that were going on in their households.

I drank whisky until three in the morning and rehashed the cycle of events. A period of severe stress followed, comprising negotiations, supporting team members and battling the change cycle together.

Many people describe redundancy like grief. You think you are fine and then out of nowhere feelings of loss wash over you and stop you in your tracks. I found this to be true.

This was my first experience of redundancy, and although painful, I now see it as invaluable. Whilst I already knew the technical aspects of modern senior job-seeking such as presenting excellent CVs, leveraging LinkedIn and selling yourself at interview, I now also understand the emotional journey that inevitably accompanies it.

Ultimately, we took full ownership of *Executive Career Jump* as part of our redundancy package and started building it more seriously while job searching and using our methodologies on our job-seeking activities.

We used the situation as the perfect challenge to test the playbook we were teaching. And it worked. We generated forty-two interviews in two weeks and secured a range of lucrative consulting assignments.

As 2019 ended we made our decision-it was time to go all-in on building a brand that would eliminate job search misery and give people the tools to succeed in their career journeys.

We set out to uncover the formula for job-seeking success in the modern job market, and we went full time into growing the business through both coaching and online offerings.

The business has grown incredibly well and has exceeded our expectations. And most importantly, we have helped hundreds of senior leaders all over the world to navigate their career transitions successfully and perform at their best in the heat of job search pressure.

In this book, I have gathered the data, the insights and the techniques to provide you with a job search playbook that gives you the edge.

So, whether you have been made redundant, successfully exited, relocated, been blindsided or outmanoeuvred by that politician in the office, we have got you covered. Job searching can be a rough ride, and it takes a toll on you, your family and your confidence, particularly when you search and realise that the job market has changed beyond all recognition since you last ventured into it.

These events may feel overwhelming, but when you read this book and subsequently talk to others, you will quickly find out that everyone has their story and what you are experiencing is not uncommon.

My goal is to help you take control of your job search, achieve clarity and get your confidence back so you may use your business skills to execute on a go-to-market strategy to get you quickly back to doing what you do best.

Sound good?

Read on and let's get to work…

CHAPTER 2

The Challenges Of Modern Job Searching

As I write this book, we are going through an incredibly volatile time for the job market and for society as a whole. We have gone from record low to record high unemployment in many western markets because of the Covid-19 Pandemic, and competition for jobs is understandably fierce.

But even before the pandemic and all of its challenges, leaders who wanted to progress their career, were already struggling to navigate the job market with the same level of confidence and clarity they had enjoyed in previous years.

With this in mind, before we share our techniques and job search playbook, it's essential to understand the dynamics at play in the modern job ecosystem and to recognise what we are up against. Modern job searching for leaders is far more complex that it used to be because the game has changed dramatically.

To show these challenges, I want to tell you about Sam, who represents so many of the men and women we coach at Executive Career Jump who have a lot on their plate.

Sam's Story

Family and friends have always described Sam as a highflyer. Approximately twenty years ago, upon leaving university, Sam entered a brilliant graduate scheme with one of the world's leading brands and rotated around the organisation to learn all about the business.

Early in their career, they decided they had the ambition to climb the corporate ladder as far as they could. Sam loved the learning, working, collaborating and competing that went with career-building and they were fortunate to have amazing mentors who helped guide them to fulfil their potential.

What followed has been a successful career by anyone's standards, which was beneficial for Sam but also took a lot of effort. They received recognition, awards, team leadership and six-figure salaries, and regular overtures from headhunters and competitors offering new opportunities to tempt them to join a different enterprise.

For the past two years, Sam has been operating in a Vice President role, heading up a significant sized P&L for XYZ Plc and the work has been high pressured, and many sacrifices made in Sam's personal life. Sam's partner and children have paid the price of the promotion and would prefer Sam to be more available. Travelling and weekend work has resulted in Sam frequently feeling on the edge of burnout.

Large houses, nice cars and expensive holidays are commonplace for the family, and Sam's job has been such an integral part of their life that it is a core part of their identity.

A couple of months ago, Sam was called into a meeting and immediately laid off with no warning. No one expected this turn of events, even though they knew that XYZ Plc had struggled in recent trading conditions. Office politics, backstabbing and the fact that they were last to join and cheaper to get rid of, even though they were great at their job, made Sam angry about the way the company handled the situation.

This is the first time Sam has experienced being out of work, and they are shocked by how much the job market has changed since they left university. Sam assumed with their track record and reputation, there would be no problem in finding a suitable new position, but that hasn't been the case and Sam now feels as though they are moving further away from achieving their goal.

Mentally and emotionally it is a struggle and feels like a grieving process where they find themselves feeling angry, emotional, frustrated and exhausted.

It shocked them to receive an automated rejection every time they applied for a job online. Their network has tried to be supportive but most of their contacts are now Sam's peers so could only help if they were vacating their own position.

Given the current financial climate, there is considerable risk aversion in the senior market and so opportunities are rare, and the flashy headhunters who were all over Sam while they were in their post, are no longer interested. Sam realised that ironically, they were more in demand when they were in their role, rather than now when they are available and most need to be attractive to the market.

Sam is also troubled by their recent interview performance. In the few instances when they man-

aged to get in front of the right hiring boards, they have been anxious and have come across as needy and over-zealous. They have received no feedback specific enough to help them improve, but they instinctively know that for the first time in a long time their confidence is depleted just when they need it most.

Everybody advises Sam to do more on LinkedIn and build a "personal brand". While they understand the importance LinkedIn now plays in careers, they haven't ever put any time in to it and don't know what to do or how to do it. Because of this lack of clarity, they procrastinate before posting on LinkedIn and second-guessing what they should share, and as a result they spend their time on the platform applying for jobs rather than posting content. Sam worries, feels a loss of identity and a level of stress which affects them and their entire family. They are snappy with their children rather than enjoying the extra time together, and they can tell their partner is worried about them and the future.

The worse bit is that they have a sinking feeling that the longer this continues, the more difficult it will be to resolve.

Sounds pretty rough, right? But sadly, it's not at all uncommon. As you are reading this book, you are probably either about to start the job search process or you are somewhere in the middle and have not yet achieved the results you desire.

Don't worry—you are in the right place and we are going to help you break through the funk and start making the progress you want.

As mentioned, one of the big challenges for people in a similar position to Sam is that senior level job searching in the 2020s is completely different from how it used to be. For example, it is estimated that a whopping eighty percent of the vacancies in the senior job market are never advertised, which means they are essentially invisible to leaders seeking their next role. You can no longer just read the appointment's page in the newspaper or ring up a few contacts to solve the problem because the job search process is considerably more complex.

One of the major challenges and opportunities for jobseekers, depending on your skill set and experience, is social media. Many leaders are not social media savvy about how it can be utilised to discover the otherwise hidden opportunities, and they may never have spent much time on professional social media platforms. Starting out with a non-existent or small network on LinkedIn can understandably feel intimidating, and for this reason, in the upcoming LinkedIn chapter we will cover how to establish a Personal Brand that not only helps you to attract your dream role during the next ten weeks but that will also future-proof your career, so you will never be in this vulnerable position again.

Unfortunately, social media is not the only technology to get our heads around; digital technology is now used throughout the hiring process and candidates frequently face assessments and are confronted with Artificial Intelligence (AI) and online testing. It is a minefield when you don't know what to expect and how to navigate this unfamiliar terrain.

In this book, we share the tactics, the playbook and the success map so you can avoid the mines and tripwires along the way. All of that being said, the CV, LinkedIn and Interview Methods you will learn about in this book are irrelevant if you don't have one thing in place first: A healthy mindset.

In the next chapter, we'll dive into mindset and show you how to set yourself up for success.

CHAPTER 3

A Transformative Mindset Update

I call our state of mind, "Mindset" because it's a recognisable personal development term, but in reality, our minds are never permanently set. It just feels that way when we get stuck in a cycle of repetitive thinking. Our minds are like the most powerful piece of software ever invented, and for that reason it's transformative to understand how they work.

The great news is that your state of mind can dramatically shift with one thought, which is why our moods change so quickly. Although popular personal development would have you believe you must work hard on your mindset; working on your mindset is as futile as trying to fix the weather.

Thoughts are as transient as the rain; they will come and go whether or not you like it. Once you're aware that it's human for your state of mind to fluctuate, and you don't need to take every thought seriously, your job search and your life will feel considerably lighter.

I've noticed there are common thought patterns people get stuck in which stop them from finding their dream job.

In my client work, I frequently wish I could give jobseekers' minds' an automatic software refresh; like we do for our laptops and phones. It would instantly update their operating system and replace obsolete behaviours and limiting beliefs. My Jobseeker Version 2.0 refresh would update the mental software to support you to perform at your best during your job search rather than using your mind as a barrier to success.

Noticing the thoughts that you take seriously is the key to enjoying a more productive state of mind. If I had a magic wand, these are the thoughts I would find and replace:

FIND: Apply to job adverts all day

REPLACE WITH: Approach industry leaders all day

FIND: I have a problem

REPLACE WITH: The Interviewer has a problem

FIND: If I reach out they might judge me

REPLACE WITH: If I reach out, they might support me

FIND: Interviews are about what I say

REPLACE WITH: Interviews are about building trust

FIND: I want to impress

REPLACE WITH: I want to assess

FIND: I want achievement

REPLACE WITH: I want fulfilment

FIND: Growing bitter

REPLACE WITH: Getting better

FIND: My job status defines me

REPLACE WITH: My character defines me

Wow! If only I could press a button and update your mind right now. It would be the greatest gift I could give someone in career transition because so many leaders struggle to think in a way which benefits their job search.

Job searching is typically a tough mental test, and your mind is the most important factor in finding and securing the role you desire. As described in the previous chapter about Sam, it is easy to find yourself in a downward spiral, with your confidence eluding you, and feeling plunged into a painful grieving cycle.

Before you even think about interviewing, when you hit the job market, I recommend you give your mind time to settle. So many jobseekers throw themselves into interviews straight away before they are ready and don't perform at their best. The interviewers can sense something is off, even if they can't identify what it is, and they choose another candidate, which damages the new jobseeker's confidence when they need it most.

Job searching at a senior level differs from when you climb the ranks. For example, one unattractive behaviour is being too pushy or keen and it can translate to appearing desperate. While being keen may be endearing in a junior applicant, it is more likely to repel an interviewer who seeks an experienced, confident senior executive. In our research, the data reveals a cruel irony; the less an executive shows they need the job, the more likely they are to be hired. And this is where things can get messy and feel counter-intuitive because the more job rejections, and the more you push, the worse you perform at the next interview. It's difficult to break out of this self-perpetuating cycle and is one to avoid. In our Executive Career Jump community, we call this affliction the J.A.B.S which stands for *Job Acquisition Burnout Syndrome.*

The key to avoiding the JABS altogether is to reframe your understanding of job searching. I recommend making your primary goal *attracting your next job, rather than chasing it.* This doesn't mean inactivity; far from it—and soon I will share the Playbook with you, so you know exactly how to create your productive job search. What it means is that you'll be more effective as you go about the process, instead of devaluing yourself and drowning in anxiety.

Now let's break down the elements of the software refresh and give you more details about the common themes and what you need to be aware of and avoid.

One of the key elements is ownership. While you can't control what has happened to you to until now, you can control what you choose to do next. Having an internal locus of control and using your considerable skills on your job search are key. It is exciting and liberating to take control of your situation and to hire yourself as the CEO of your job search. Your full-time job is finding your next career move!

Another key theme is becoming comfortable being uncomfortable, or at least allowing yourself to feel uncomfortable, and understanding that it won't hurt you in the long term.

Being brave enough to share your thoughts, build a personal brand and sell yourself as the solution the market needs can be a tough mental shift, which is why I am going to help you through the process.

The humility that made you an outstanding leader while in your post, may now be the enemy of you attracting your next role. It's time to release your fear of "getting out there", and instead practice promoting yourself within your network so they are aware of the tremendous skills and experience you offer, as opportunities arise.

Change is tough, and while most of us accept this as a fundamental truth, it is helpful to view this free time you have between roles as an opportunity. It's a great chance to spend more time with the people you care about, to learn new skills, and to focus on your health and fitness. In order to perform better you must feel better, and that is why the *"grow better, not bitter"* part of this chapter is such an important message. When I work with Executive Career Jump private clients, and in our community, I notice how obsessed people can become with their former boss and company. It makes it more difficult to attract the dream role we desire, when we feel bitter and spend our days wallowing in a cycle of polluted thinking.

Attracting a new role is like attracting a new partner after a painful romantic break-up. It's unlikely you'll fall in love again until you relax enough to notice the people and opportunities under your nose.

By letting go of the past, you give yourself the freedom to move forward, and while I can't do this for you, I can point you in the right direction. Noticing any bitterness, and deciding to stop dwelling on the past, and to live in the moment, is a giant step towards true mental freedom which will serve you well in every area of your life.

I have known jobseekers spend months stewing, over-analysing, and obsessing about their ex-employer. They think and talk about them, and waste their precious energy looking through the rear-view mirror rather than at the road ahead.

If this sounds familiar, I encourage you to decide today to draw a line beneath the past and give yourself permission to move on. Whatever happened is not in your control, and while it may still feel hurtful, we don't serve ourselves well by focussing on it, and continually living in the past.

In the next chapter we are going to move into helping you gain clarity on what you should focus on in attracting your next role.

Let us guide you to understanding what you really want to do next in your career.

Ready? Read on…

CHAPTER 4

Understanding What You Want

One of the positive things about finding yourself on the job market is being able to reflect and work out exactly what you want to do next. Getting clarity on your next career step is important as you need to know what type of opportunity you wish to attract with your go-to market plan.

I recommend you take notes to get the most out of this section.

Let's run through a quick yet profound discovery exercise to help you understand what you want:

1. What is most important to you right now from an overall life perspective?

At Executive Career Jump we don't talk about "work life balance", we talk about "work life integration". This is identifying a working pattern and purpose that meets your priorities and helps contribute to you achieving a satisfying level of fulfilment.

Write down what is most important to you now.

Is it family time, fitness, career progression or freedom? Whatever comes to mind, capture it, as this is a key part of working out how you will market yourself and what you want to attract in your career.

2. **Where and when have you been most productive in your career?**

We have all had periods in our career when we have felt productive, impactful, and like we were making significant progress. Some sport stars call this a "flow state" or refer to being "in the zone". While we might never feel quite the same buzz as a competitor at Wimbledon or Wembley, we have all felt productive and fulfilled at some point.

When was this for you? Why do you think it occurred? What were the circumstances? Note it all down.

3. **What type of leader got the best out of you?**

The question is not "What type of leader do you like working with, the most?". These are two very different questions. For example, the leader who got the best out of you may have been a proponent of "tough love", and difficult to work with. Use your self-awareness to work out what you need and want from your next leader.

I always urge people to pick a leader rather than a job. The leader you work for is the most important factor in your fulfilment and well-being, so give this some serious thought and write it down.

4. **What type of business problems do you solve best?**

Most jobseekers only talk about what they have done, rather than the pain points or the business problems that they solve. This is an error. By thinking about what kinds of problems you are good at solving, you position yourself as relevant to the marketplace, and it's simpler to work out where you are most suited to work next. You also find that a lot of the problems you are good at solving are industry agnostic and transferable.

Note whatever comes to mind and if you're not sure, then ask people who have worked with you and do some "self-referencing". This is the process of reviewing references on previous work and asking colleagues to talk you through what they see as your strengths.

Many of our strengths come naturally to us, so having others point them out can be revealing.

5. In terms of money and location, what constraining factors are at play for your job search?

It is important to approach your job search with a sensible mix of both optimism and realism. Many of us have constraining factors at play, whether financial or practical, such as where we are based.

Take a pragmatic view and note the realistic picture of how far you would be willing to travel and what you need to earn to maintain a minimum acceptable lifestyle in your next job.

What size of organisation and working style is important to you in your next role?

There is no easy route to fulfilment in your career (despite what the "gurus" tell you) but you do have options. In the new world of work, many people plan their own work patterns, and the big companies no longer have a monopoly on the best talent pools.

Here are the options in terms of career direction for you to consider and the typical pros and cons of each:

Big company

PROS: Stability, good employee benefits, training, peers and colleagues.
CONS: Politics, lack of impact, slow to make decisions and change.

Small company

Pros: Your relevance and impact, faster pace of change, growth journey and breadth of role.

Cons: Firefighting, Founder interference, limited cash flow and instability.

Interim/consulting/portfolio career

Pros: Variety, fewer politics, freedom, tax efficiency, ability to be objective and double down on strengths.
Cons: Feast and famine, high level of customer demands and responsibility and some risk.

Your own start-up

Pros: Bring your vision, mission, and values to life. Amazing highs.
Cons: Crushing lows and high stress, poor work-life balance and high risk.

You can win big and get fulfilment in any of the above or even try all of them at various points in your career.

For this exercise, note which of the above options is your primary focus now.

1. What would you do if you weren't afraid?

Fear holds us back in our career, and in my experience most people are never brave enough to do what they truly want. I always knew I wanted to work for myself, but only took the plunge because of circumstances rather than by my own design.

This is one of my favourite questions to ask. Jot down what springs to mind.

2. Who do you envy?

When trying to identify what you want, envy is an underrated emotion. It's an obvious clue about what you desire and so is worth investigating.

When was the last time you felt professional envy? What do you think conjured up that emotion? What is it that person has that you want?

Being honest about who and what you envy is your intuition guiding you, and you can harness this powerful emotion positively to lead you toward your next big career move.

Now take the time to review your notes and pull together a mission statement that clarifies the type of opportunity you want to secure next.

Here is an example:

The role I will attract is working within an organisation that is small and has a leadership team with high expectations but that also empowers its people.

The organisation is experiencing challenges in their business with their customer retention and sales, and the value and experience I bring is my ability to be both creative and analytical in driving growth. The work pattern will be a combination of working from home, working with colleagues in the office, and visiting customers.

I am looking for a role working for an organisation based in the North West of England and pays a minimum of £80,000. The role I am targeting could be on a consultancy or a permanent basis because the way I am paid is less important to me.

I see this as a five-year journey that will elevate me to board level.

It feels great to have absolute clarity on what you want, so I urge you to take it seriously.

In the next chapter, we'll talk about how to use systems and processes to achieve your mission statement.

CHAPTER 5

The Go-To-Market Plan

Hope is not a strategy, yet without a robust plan, many senior job-seekers rely on applying to job adverts and get hooked on what we at Executive Career Jump call hope-ium. It's a potent substance, and you may have already fallen into this common trap.

Why? Well, because applying for jobs makes you feel busy and although you may take lots of action; being busy is rarely enough to get the results you want. As always, it's about what you put into the time, not how much busy-time you spend.

If this shocks you because you thought you were doing the right thing, I'm sorry to be the bearer of bad news, but I don't want you to waste any more of your precious time with busy work that is unlikely to land you your dream role.

Unfortunately, responding to job adverts doesn't cut it in today's job market. The latest data reveals that there is less than a one percent chance of getting an interview following a traditional job application.

It's difficult to believe so if you're not convinced, consider this: It's estimated that eighty-five percent of senior level job opportunities lurk in what we call "the hidden job market." They aren't advertised and so are invisible to the traditional job seeker.

I hope you now see the importance of adopting a more productive way of identifying your next role.

Senior hires still occur, but they are behind the scenes, which is why it is so frustrating and seems out of reach when you don't know where or how to find them.

The good news is that once you implement the Go-To Market Plan, I'll share with you in this chapter, you see you are already equipped for a successful job search.

Let's now check you into what I call "Job Advert Rehab" and show you exactly how to fine-tune your thinking and start using your considerable business skills for your job search.

Let's Begin

Job seekers must first be aware of senior vacancies. Then they need to know how to identify these opportunities through advocates personal recommendations and the direct approach, instead of the old way of applying to job adverts.

Most senior leaders I have helped to find their next dream role, even in the toughest of financial climates, learned to leverage their networks and capitalise on other routes to the job market.

To accelerate and succeed in your job search, you must execute a multi-channel strategy. I recommend you tackle your job search with all the exuberance and skill that you plan to bring to your next role. It's inspiring to view finding your perfect job as *the job*, rather than as a tiresome inconvenience. With this subtle yet powerful mind-shift, you'll bring fresh energy to your "job" and it will permeate all of your activities. This way, when you reach the point of interviews, you'll be excited rather than exhausted, which makes all the difference to your success.

Like any problem you have faced in your business life, you can break your job search down into key activities, the results of which compound over time to help you reach your goal.

Leaders must cut through the noise to attract their new role, and for that you need to put four foundational elements in place for your solid go-to-market plan.

The Three Foundational Elements

1. A job search activity tracker
2. A high-impact and ATS compliant CV
3. A diary or calendar

Now let's explore the three key foundational elements, starting with number one, a job search activity tracker.

What gets measured is more likely to get done, so for your job search to be a success, you'll need an activity tracker to log your daily activities. Trello and HubSpot are popular with our clients, and there are many other fancy software packages to monitor progress, but if you prefer, you can choose to keep it simple with an Excel spreadsheet.

Let's use Excel for this example. The first task is to save a file as *Job Hunt* because you're going to be proactively hunting for your dream job.

At the bottom of the Excel sheet, create five tabs. These tabs represent the proven five core roots to finding employment, based on statistics and job search data.

Name the five tabs

Tab one
Work-in-Progress

Tab two
Network KPIs

Tab three
Recruiters and Headhunters

Tab four
The Dream 20

Tab five
Content

Now let's look at how to utilise the tabs to attract opportunity and to organise your job search:

Tab one

Work-in-Progress is to record job applications, interviews and roles for which you are currently being considered. It's helpful to "traffic light" the jobs, based on the stage of each application. Red jobs are for when you've made an application, amber is for when you've had a response, and green is for when you're at interviewing stage or beyond.

This is a really important tab because it allows you, in a snapshot, to review your job pipeline and to work out how you might get an edge at each stage. The two things to focus on in your Work-in-Progress tab are to find out how you can drive urgency and what you can do to persuade relevant individuals to take you to the next level.

There are various techniques such as using references and getting people to refer you or to advocate your application. But at every stage, you need to be thinking, 'how do I move this forward?'

Tab two

Network contacts, or, as we call them in the Executive Career Jump ecosystem, KPIs. These aren't the KPIs familiar from previous job roles. In networking, KPIs stands for key people of influence, so for this tab, document all the people in your network who you consider to be key people of influence. They may or may not be people who can directly hire you, but they are well-connected. The aim is to tap into your network of KPIs, so you are the first person who comes to mind when an appropriate requirement comes up in conversation or hits their desk.

When you're reviewing your network to identify KPIs, select people who are well-networked. They may be friends, family, suppliers, customers, former colleagues or bosses. These are the relationships to nurture.

The key to getting value from your KPIs is what's known as the "Law of Reciprocity". Reciprocity makes the senior job market tick along, and the reason it works so well is that the more value you add, the more people willingly help you. Rather than approaching your network like most people do; looking to extract value from relationships, instead get creative about ways you can stay front of mind with your network KPIs by solving problems for them.

For example, consider which connections would be useful for them, or utilise your skills to help them. Remember, what's easy for you is often difficult for others. When you help people, they feel compelled to return the favour. The more you pay into your senior network and ecosystem, the more others will look after you. And this shift of adding value first, rather than trying only to extract it, will set you up for success.

Tab three

Document all the recruiters and headhunters with whom you already have a relationship. As with KPIs, the key with recruiters is to make sure they remember you, you're registered on their databases, and that you keep in touch. I recommend you aim to get to know ten recruiters well. Make the effort to connect and help them with referrals, share market information and make sure you're on their list of people they would refer when they receive new opportunities. The goal is to become the person they think of and call first.

Finding recruiters is simple: they spend a lot of time on LinkedIn. Search for recruiters using the people tab in the LinkedIn search bar, and then drill down using filters by location, industry or specialism. I recommend you aim to build your recruiter list to between thirty and fifty to make sure you've got your market covered and you can find ten who become your powerful marketing channel.

Headhunters are frequently the conduit to the hidden market we talked about earlier, because they get engaged to fill unadvertised positions.

Tab four

Dream 20 is an aspirational list of twenty companies you would most like to work with next, based on location, mission, product, service, or all of these criteria. If you're in business development, you'll recognise that the approach we take to Dream 20 is similar to an account-based selling strategy.

Map out the key leaders in each business, including the HR Director, and get on their radar.

On this tab, write the company names in one row, and then write several job titles across the top and start to populate the sheet. Use LinkedIn, Google, Companies House, and whatever channels occur to you to map out your Dream 20, so you know where to focus your energy.

LinkedIn is my favourite channel for this as you can follow the companies on LinkedIn, like and comment on their content, and be an advocate of what they're doing. By championing the companies, they'll notice you and you will make a positive impression.

Some of our clients have had success writing to their dream companies. As people don't receive letters much anymore, posting a letter with your resume and credentials can be a powerful way to stand out and cut through the busy online noise. Your Dream 20 work is all about building cadence and traction with the companies that you would most like to work for.

Tab five

This is your Content tab. In this tab, capture content ideas that come to you as you go about the business of your job search. Ideas typically float into your mind when you least expect them, so be ready to jot them down for when you're ready to share content. There's no need to pressure yourself as ideas arrive effortlessly when you relax, especially when you pay attention and don't miss them! You'll get what you need when you need it. That's how the mind works, so harness this natural mind power for your job search.

We will get into the full personal branding playbook later, but I'm including a content tab in the tracker, so you can capture more ideas as you track your data.

After you post any content, track how many views, comments and likes you receive, so you get a feel for the posts that resonate with your audience. If you're new to posting content, you might feel out of your depth at first, but remember this is part of your new job and will help you achieve your goal. Like everything, it will become easier as you grow accustomed to sharing and posting. The more you post content that resonates with your network, the more visible your content will be, so it's a virtuous circle, and before long it will feel as simple as making a cup of coffee.

Posting and tracking content is a great way to stand out and to measure the success of your personal branding efforts. If you leverage these channels correctly, you are going to get plenty of attention, traction and targeted leads. Once you begin to generate leads, you need a high-impact CV which converts opportunities into interviews rather than being overlooked and discarded on the CV slush pile.

A High-Impact and ATS compliant CV

This is the second foundational element. People dread CV writing and for good reason when they don't know how to create a CV that is high impact and meets the expectations of today's marketplace.

I imagined we wouldn't need CVs for much longer, but alas, they are still essential to secure new roles. There are hundreds of opinions on what a good CV looks like, but we base our method on the shocking research that most hiring leaders only review a CV for under eight seconds. This eight-second research tallies with my own experience as a headhunter when I witnessed CEOs, MDs and other time-crunched leaders scanning CVs and deciding in seconds who was suitable for an interview.

On almost all occasions, much to my frustration, they ignored most of my Headhunter notes and insights, and continued to scan instead. With this in mind, here are the six CV rules that will serve you well when creating your own high-impact CV.

Six CV Rules

Rule one: Keep to less than three pages. Three pages is the absolute maximum you need, and ironically, the more experienced you are, the shorter your CV. You need to show people you know how to communicate in a concise and impactful way, because that's going to be key to the leadership role that you want to attract.

Rule two: Cut down on details of your personal profile. Nine times out of ten, when I pick up a senior person's CV, the profile at the top is far too long, which is the old-style format. They typically comprise boring blocks of text full of generic buzzwords. I recommend you write a concise introduction at the top of your CV and save the premium space for the details that will create the wow factor and make people want to hire you.

Rule three: Make sure you have your most impressive and relevant career achievements in the first section of your CV in an easy-to-read format. This way they won't get lost in the details of each role.

Pick the top five that you most want your future boss to know, so as soon as they pick up the document you make an instant high impact and make it on to the "Yes" pile.

Rule four: The skill section is where you detail what you bring to the table and the competencies that match the jobs for which you're applying. These could be a combination of technical and behavioural competencies, and if you're applying for a specific role, it's best to tailor this section to use the exact words used in the job brief.

This is the second key section of your CV, and when you do this, you're already off to a strong start. You've avoided the usual wordy personal profile, listed your key career achievements, and your top skills, before going into more detail about your previous roles.

Rule five: Own your career history and be proud of it. When you fill in a summary of each job in your career history, only cover the past ten to fifteen years to avoid age discrimination. Talk about what 'you' did rather than what 'we' did and use positive descriptive words to show the full impact you had and how you drove certain outcomes. Don't hold back on outlining the scope and scale of what you achieved.

Rule six: ATS stands for Applicant Tracking System. The ATS System is the AI (Artificial Intelligence) behind modern job adverts and helps companies sift through responses. Many companies receive over one thousand applications to individual roles, so AI is used to save time and money to find the top five percent of potentially suitable applicants.

There are several considerations in understanding what the bots look for and how they work so you can beat them. Bots don't like fancy formatting, so while your high-impact CV might look impressive with company logos and other visuals, it's unlikely to get through. Bots also don't like hyperlinks, so keep to plain text and clean formatting to improve your chances of getting it past the AI bots.

Write a CV that adheres to these six simple rules and it will command instant attention from the right people and do the job it is designed to do, which is convert into interview opportunities. It must be clean, easy to digest, tailored to the specific requirements of each role and high-impact.

Writing your CV can cause overwhelm, so with this chapter I've included a complimentary example of a high-impact ATS compliant CV for you to model.

Download it here: www.execcareerjump.com/ats-free-template

This brings us to the final foundational element of our go-to-market strategy, which is your diary or calendar.

Research shows that having structure and routine helps jobseekers enjoy better mental health during what can be a tough period. In our Executive Career Jump community, members share that they enjoy organising their diary like the CEO of their own job search, as if they were still in a role. This is a positive move and we encourage it; whether you use an online calendar or a paper diary, organising your time around the tasks in your activity tracker is a good discipline to maintain.

Some members even build in a fake commute, which involves getting up and ready for the day before going for a twenty-minute walk and then arriving back home as if they are arriving at work. This has several benefits: daily exercise in fresh air and to prepare them for work mode.

It's tempting to lie in, and not be productive because you're at home, so the fake commute gives many people a simple structure to start their day.

We also encourage scheduling plenty of time in your calendar for the three Fs: friends, family and fitness. Being productive in your job search is critical but having more free time than you usually have, is also a wonderful chance to work on yourself and to nurture your relationships.

It's unlikely you will have as much free time for the three Fs once you're in your new role, so don't miss what may be a rare opportunity to enjoy a more flexible schedule.

Now you have your Go-To Market Plan and know how to take control of your job search, I encourage you to give yourself permission to enjoy some guilt-free time off around your job search commitments.

The content tab mentioned above is just one part of the digital element of the playbook I will share with you to make it simpler to implement your plan. Digital platforms represent a once in a career opportunity, and this is what we will cover in more detail in the next chapter.

CHAPTER 6

Generating Job Opportunities Through Your Network

As a leader on the job market your goal is simple: to be the most referred candidate in your network.

To achieve this, you have to be front of mind so that when people who know you are in conversation when an opportunity is mentioned; you are the first person they recommend.

At this point you should have clarity on the type of role you want, and a go-to-market strategy in place to attract it. As described earlier, and worth repeating to make sure you've fully grasped the significance of the hidden job market: *the vast majority of senior job roles are not secured through adverts.*

With this in mind, it's time to leverage a vital channel: Your network.

When describing and helping you to create the Job Search Tracker, we talked about KPIs and headhunters as key routes to market. This chapter is about leveraging the relationships you have and continuing to grow your network as you navigate your job search.

There are two powerful forces which fuel the job ecosystem at a senior level: Advocacy and Reciprocity, which I understood when I was a head-hunter.

Candidates were sent, who had been directly recommended to the leadership team at the hiring company, and I was instructed to prioritise them in our assessment.

We live in a world where we outsource a lot of our decision-making processes. People consult reviews before making a purchase such as booking a hotel room, and of course hiring decisions are no different. The pressure to make good senior level hiring decisions is significant, so any way of reducing the risk through trusted contacts helps companies feel more in control of their recruitment.

For this reason, I recommend you leverage "Advocacy" to your advantage and we'll explore how to do so shortly.

Reciprocity is the second force. People don't enjoy feeling indebted, so the more you add value to people rather than extract it, the better you will position yourself, and the more job leads will naturally flow your way.

Let's look at how we can generate reciprocity and people to advocate us through our network and by partnering with headhunters and recruiters: KPIs (Key People of Influence)

Go back to your Job Search Tracker and have another brainstorm to make sure your initial list of network contacts is complete. Have you listed all the well-connected people you know?

I recommend you aim for twenty-thirty people to ensure a generous pool of contacts to nurture. They could be previous colleagues, suppliers, customers or even friends and family. They don't have to be people who could hire you directly—they might be people who could refer you.

I've found that what most leaders on the market do (which is a big mistake) is to whiz over their CV to these influential people and say, "Let me know if you have any jobs". This is understandable but it's also lazy and transactional, so they're just as quickly forgotten, and this brief interaction is not conducive to building reciprocity.

Instead, what you need to do is find a way to add value.

Here are some great ways I have seen our coaching clients add value and stay front of mind of the people in their network:

Offer Your Time

Many leaders are lonely and have a lot on their plate so why not offer your contacts some of your time to help bounce ideas around and help them reach clarity?

It's great for you because it refreshes your skills and keeps you close to what's happening in the market, and it's also great for the other person to access free coaching or consulting from an experienced professional.

It could result in further consulting work and will certainly help move you closer to becoming the most referred candidate in your marketplace.

You can use a simple note like the following example:

> "Hi xxx
>
> I hope you and your family are well.
>
> For the first time in a long time, I find myself with both capacity and free time. I would imagine you currently have a lot on your plate, so I'm extending a special invitation to you.
>
> Do you fancy having a thirty-minute coffee meet up on a video call to work through something you are grappling with in your business? If you feel I could add value, I'd be thrilled to do so, and look forward to catching up.
>
> Would love to hear from you.
>
> Regards,
> (Name)"

Be A Connector

It's time to play matchmaker!

Are there people on your KPI list who could add significant value to each other?

If so, go ahead and make the introductions.

Do it via email or set up a channel on LinkedIn message and connect them up.

Playing the role of connector is powerful and helps you establish yourself as a go-to-person in your marketplace and also gives you a simple strategy to nurture those relationships. You'll feel good by helping others as you help yourself, so it's a win-win.

Offer Your Insights

A great activity to focus on is to work out how you can use your skills to provide valuable insights to busy people in your network.

Any service that would usually cost money can lead to referrals and consulting opportunities. You could send them over with a brief note or better still, contact them first to see what they're struggling with.

Here are some good service examples:

- Product Ideas
- Website Review
- Customer Journey
- Employee Value Proposition (EVP) review
- Cost Reduction Plan
- Business Case

And there are many more, so get your thinking cap on and get busy providing value, and it will come back to you tenfold. I've found it to be true that the more you help people get what they want, the more chance you will get what you want!

Working With Headhunters

The other key tab on your job search activity tracker is the one which documents the consultant names and companies you are in contact with in the headhunting and recruitment industry.

First, let's clear up the difference between headhunters and recruitment consultants. Broadly speaking, headhunters get paid up front by the client to work on a particular search project. They work at the more senior end of the market in a particular industry, such as, Technology, Manufacturing or FMCG, and are typically partner-led professional services firms.

Recruitment Consultants work in the mid and entry levels and only get paid on results. They are more open to approach, and they build large databases of people. They specialise in role types rather than specific industries, for example: Finance, HR, change managers, and are typically either small boutiques or major plc sized international businesses.

The market is fragmented, but if you engage in the way I recommend, both recruitment consultants and headhunters hold the keys to accessing the hidden market of non-advertised jobs.

Recruitment consultants get a bad-rap and often for good reason, but having worked in the industry for many years, I can tell you that the best ones in your market are invaluable.

You probably know some top recruiters in your market already, so make sure they are on your list, you have sent them your CV, and you are connected on LinkedIn. It is also worth trying to build out your list through a LinkedIn search. Type "recruitment consultant" or "executive search" into the search bar and refine the search using the filters to find a collection of profiles to add to your network.

Mistakes to avoid when developing your relationship with recruiters:

- Forgetting that recruiters are paid by and work for the hiring client, not you.

If you need a Career Coach, then hire one, rather than expecting free services.
- Trying to cut the head-hunter or recruiter out of the process.

    This will destroy any chance of developing trust with the head-hunter. Show recruiters you value their input, and work with them on recruitment processes, not against them.
- Telling recruiters about other opportunities for which you are interviewing. Unfortunately, some recruiters will chase those roles as "leads" which could diminish your chances of getting the offer.

    Pass on leads to recruiters for roles you are no longer interested in but keep your current application role data and your pipeline to yourself.

It is worth asking other executives in your market which head-hunter they had a pleasant experience with in their latest job search and asking them to refer you directly. This is another example of the power of Advocacy and will usually get your CV on to the top of the pile and increase the chances of an exploratory call if you're a suitable match for the head-hunter.

I urge you to get busy building Advocacy and Reciprocity to create an ecosystem where you feel great because you are adding value while uncovering ideal opportunities. It is not only more fun than surfing through endless job adverts; it is also much more productive and will pay off long after you've secured your next role.

These small but important moves compound over time and remember you are only ever one recommendation away from the interview that gets you in to your new exciting role, so trust the process and do the work!

In the next chapter, I'll take you through how to generate job opportunities online.

CHAPTER 7

Generating Job Opportunities Online

As I mentioned earlier, the once in-demand job pages in newspapers have become obsolete. In their place are several digital channels that offer the opportunity to access not only advertised roles but also the so called "hidden job market".

These are the roles which either have an incumbent in post, confidentiality in place, or a discreet process underway.

Estimates suggest that at a senior level eighty-five percent of executive roles are in this hidden world, behind the scenes, and only accessible via personally branded networking. If you aren't active in online networking and haven't yet created your personal brand, this realisation may be a shock and you can see how easy it is for someone to be busy applying for jobs but unable to attract interviews. At this point many people become disillusioned and they slide in to *Job Acquisition Burnout Syndrome.*

If the term "Personal Branding" is new to you, or you've never had to think much about it before, you may now wonder what on earth it's all about.

And if in the past decade you have noticed the growing emphasis on building a personal brand when job hunting or increasing sales, and feel intimidated, then you're not alone. Prior to the last couple of years, I was uneasy about it too, but once I began strategically building a personal brand for myself and my clients, I was blown away by the benefits. Not only was I able to grow my new business purely through LinkedIn, I also invested and helped found a personal branding agency (Klowt.io), adding over fifty-thousand followers in just twelve months and I am now regularly booked to speak about Personal Branding.

It's been an incredible journey. I started out as a guy with no marketing experience, who was vocal about my dislike of social media and some might say has a face for podcasts!

What caused my change of heart? I realised personal branding had moved on from being an ego-driven activity to a strategic imperative. It was as simple as that.

And my company's data and client results speak for themselves. In the last twelve months over fifty percent of our career coaching clients who have received job offers, attracted their job via LinkedIn, or through another type of online networking using their personal brand. Almost all of these clients were reluctant to begin the process but are now enthusiastic advocates after experiencing positive results.

What is Personal Branding?

Personal branding is a deliberate strategy to position yourself as an expert in your field by sharing relevant content and ultimately advancing your job search prospects. The good news is your timing is spot on: there is now a once-in-a-career opportunity to build a personal brand via LinkedIn that will not only help you attract job opportunities in the short term but will support your long-term career too.

The growth of LinkedIn has been unbelievable. From a small professional networking site in 2002 to having over seven hundred million members in 2020, generating nine billion weekly post impressions, it has developed into an ecosystem where people buy, sell and source the best jobs on the market.

What makes LinkedIn such an incredible platform, (and no, I am not on commission!) is that it has an unrivalled level of what marketers call "organic reach". Put another way, this means that when you write a post on LinkedIn, there is still an opportunity to grow your audience and for other people to see your post without having to "pay to play" for the exposure, like other platforms where the once impressive organic reach has significantly declined. And with the current and growing trend of remote working, your next employer is probably online and more accessible than ever.

Many people experience anxiety about networking via social media, and I understand why. LinkedIn can feel like an intimidating place when you don't feel at home, but of all the social media platforms you will find it the most professional, welcoming and courteous, so fear not. I urge you to put aside any pride, ego and worries about what others will think and take the plunge.

Shortly I will share some insights from our Playbook that have helped people get hired using LinkedIn, but first I'll share common pitfalls and errors people make.

Traps to Avoid

Trap one: Not Focusing on Your Target Audience

To ensure your online networking and personal branding activities are moving in the right direction, know who you are looking to attract. Great online networking is about helping others rather than purely trying to extract value for yourself. When many senior jobseekers share content, their LinkedIn postings aren't focused and don't convey their core message.

When you did the exercises in the Understanding What You Want chapter, I hope you gained clarity around the type of role you wish to attract as part of your job searching campaign. Before you share content online, you need to think about the person who will hire you: your future boss or your future customer if you're in business.

This is known as a "buyer persona" exercise which people undertake when working in marketing, so they can successfully target a certain customer group with a laser focus. I recommend you apply the same approach to your job search.

Here is how to do it:

Step 1–Name them

For example: My target audience is Jobseeker Sam.

Step 2–Describe them

Here's mine: Sam is an experienced leader who is struggling to navigate the current job market.

Step 3–Write down three of their pain points

For example:

- *They don't have clarity around what to do to conduct their job search effectively*
- *They don't know how to access the hidden job market*
- *They're experiencing a crisis of confidence that negatively affects their attitude and interview performance*

Step 4–Write down what they most want

For example, Jobseeker Sam wants clarity, confidence, and a competitive advantage.

Keep this information handy throughout your job search. As I mentioned earlier, some people put a picture of their ideal boss on their desk, so they have them in their mind and can write to them specifically when they post content.

1. Writing in a "Vanilla" style

This is such a common error, particularly in those who come from a more corporate or professional services background. The first thing I tell anyone who is starting their LinkedIn journey is to "write as you talk". A caveat here is to always take a moment to read through what you've written before hitting the publish button, so there are no glaring grammatical errors. Being authentic is the key to success, but you are writing with the goal of attracting your ideal boss or customer, and you don't want to turn them off with misspellings and poor English.

However, your LinkedIn post isn't an academic research paper but a conversation starter. People buy people and the more authentic the post, the better so that when you move to the next step, the "real you" will be congruent with your personally branded content. Always showcase your best self as that shows the attitude your future boss or client will assume you'll bring to work. In our work at Executive Career Jump, we call this, "Authentic Professionalism."

2. Inconsistency

Consistent activity is the key to building momentum on LinkedIn. Many people 'give LinkedIn a go' but don't make it a habit and so they don't tap into the hidden job opportunities. Remember to refer to your diary and activity planner in the Go-To-Market Plan chapter, and schedule in regular posts so posting becomes a habit.

3. Treating LinkedIn like a "Black Book".

LinkedIn is not only about accepting invitations and interacting with people you know, it is a powerful ecosystem within which the more you pay in the more you get out.

Accept invitations to connect from people you don't know because even if they're not of immediate interest to you, you don't know who they know. Leave thoughtful comments on other people's posts and reach out to relevant contacts to add them to your network. There is no benefit to your job search in playing small on the LinkedIn platform.

Understanding and implementing these four key components will give you a competitive advantage over others who are in the market and are competing for the same roles as you.

Your Profile Page

Your profile on LinkedIn serves as a shop window for your ideal employer. It is critical to position yourself so recruiters who are hiring can find you, and so your value is immediately obvious to anyone who visits, or whom you invite to connect. Your profile must be both impactful and buzzword rich.

There is a tonne of advice out there on how to optimise your profile page and it can be conflicting.

To help you cut through the overwhelm, here is my simple 10 Point Checklist:

1. Add profile picture that is a recent headshot
2. Add an engaging banner photo
3. Write a headline which includes the role titles for which you want to be found
4. Update your job search preferences
5. Write the About Section in your profile and include the pain point and problems you solve for your ideal employer, your skills and the keywords for which you wish to be found.
6. Build out the work experience section and ensure all descriptions are keyword rich.
7. Ask people you have worked with for a recommendation to add to your profile.
8. Use the pronunciation feature to add your name and voice to your profile.
9. Upload CV and supporting documents as attachments.
10. Add your contact details to encourage people to reach out.

Now your "shop window" is suitably dressed, you are almost ready to add connections and post content to drive relevant eyeballs (and job enquiries) to your page.

Before you do so, you need to understand how the algorithm works.

The LinkedIn Algorithm

Algorithms change all the time on social platforms, and anyone claiming they can hack the algorithm is probably making false claims. There are however certain things you can do to optimise your post.

In my experience of working with clients and in posting my content, I have developed a framework that gives your post the best chance of avoiding negative ranking and not sinking to the bottom of the newsfeed.

LinkedIn Post Optimisation

When you post on the platform, your post is initially only shown to a few people. How many people comment on your post in the first ninety minutes, determines how many others will then be shown your content. I call this first hour after you post, "the golden hour".

To maximise the impact of your post during the golden hour, don't do a "hit and run", but stick around to nurture your post after sharing, with an aim of encouraging likes and comments. Your comments also count, so add some comments with questions in your posts to encourage debate, and when you receive a reply make sure you respond to each comment, particularly within the golden hour.

A major issue with the algorithm is that it doesn't like posts which contain any type of link to other sites, including email addresses. It's understandable because LinkedIn's goal is to keep people in their ecosystem, so why would they promote something that will lead people away from their platform? When you grasp the basics, it makes it easy to leverage LinkedIn. If you want to share an article, email address, or drive traffic to another website, remember to add it to the comments rather than within the body of your post, and then you will avoid this issue.

Now you understand the power of engagement in the "golden hour" and how to make sure you don't get ranked down, let's look at WHAT to post and HOW?

What to Post?

One of the major blocks people suffer from when trying to get into the habit of posting content is a blank mind; they don't know what to say. Once you start, you'll see that content ideas are all around you, and one of the best ways to create engaging content is to consume content. By reading books, listening to podcasts and engaging in social media, the creative cogs begin to turn, and ideas arrive naturally.

You can also come up with ideas on what to post by referring to the exercise we did earlier on your target audience and the pain that you solve.

What does your target audience care about?

Keep your content radar alert when you watch the news, read the paper, or in networking discussions and build a pipeline of relevant topics on your phone.

How to Post

There are three post formats you can use on LinkedIn:

Long Form Blogs

This is when you publish an article of between eight-hundred and twelve-hundred words and include an image. The engagement on long form blogs isn't high but they add credibility to your profile, potentially feed search algorithms and are a useful tool for networking—which we'll cover in more detail in a later chapter.

Vlogs

These are video updates of between ninety and three-hundred seconds where you record a video on your phone and share it. The engagement is typically high because people enjoy seeing people on video, which fast tracks the "know, like, trust" factor. I recommend doing videos and if you want to add subtitles there are various free apps available.

Micro-Blogs

This format is dynamite and is the simple method I've used to generate over eleven million views of my content this year alone, with which I help jobseekers attract new opportunities.

A micro-blog is simply a plain text post (not an article) that is less than thirteen-hundred characters and spaced out, so it is easy to digest. The organic reach on these types of posts is huge, and it is well worth overcoming any initial resistance and getting into the habit of posting regularly.

Each type of content plays a unique role, and in my experience and that of my clients, a blended approach with a majority of micro-blogs is most effective for a LinkedIn content-posting-strategy.

Here are some ideas on the types of posts that work well in generating opportunities for leaders on the move:

A Flare Post

You may be relieved to hear I'm not referring to a photo of you wearing questionable jeans…but the type of flare you fire into the sky to alert people.

By writing a Flare post on LinkedIn where you "park your pride" and make it clear you have the capacity for new clients or are seeking a new role, it may surprise you to find you attract support, consulting opportunities or even your ideal job.

Sharing a flare post is a great way to start your personal branding and job search journey.

It is important that the flare post is positive and has a clear call to action but doesn't sound desperate because that repels people and will have the opposite effect to what you desire.

Here is an example template for you to tweak:

> "Hi everyone,
>
> Wanted to share an update on my next move. By now, you may know that after nearly x years, I left XYZ a few weeks ago.
> I am truly happy and thankful to have met so many great friends and worked with such a diverse group of colleagues during this time. My last role managing the team was an incredible experience. Together we built a great group and achieved so much.
> In some ways it was really sad to leave, but I am now eager to take the next step.
> So, what's next?
> I want to continue to do what I do best: help companies transform their xxx and lead their teams to deliver growth and an improved x.
> I'm already in discussion with some very interesting companies, so stay tuned!
> If any of you have suggestions on opportunities, please send them my way. For now, I wish you all the best, keep safe and stay healthy.
>
> Thanks
> (Name)"

Make the post your own so it sounds like you, as that will resonate with people in your network.

Good luck with your own Flare post, and remember to monitor your post, employ the "golden hour" and reply to any comments.

If you're new to personal branding and posting content, don't give up if you don't attract many responses initially. It can take a while for LinkedIn to make your content visible, and for people to engage with you, which is why you need different types of content.

When helping others to create their content-posting-strategy, and when posting my content, I have found that three types of post significantly out-perform others.

My company went back through all the data and we categorised these posts into Three "C's": Championing, Commentary and Capability posts. If you consistently share these types of posts, you will quickly gain traction.

Championing Post

Championing posts get the highest engagement and are when you champion a cause or an audience. You may be "calling out" a problematic issue that exists in your industry or offering recognition.

To uncover championing post ideas, answer the following questions:

1. What do people in your market feel but not say out loud?
2. Who doesn't get recognition in your market?
3. What could you write that you feel strongly about, that people might want to share?

Commentary Posts

Here are some questions to inspire this type of post:

1. What is the most surprising stat or skill you have learnt recently?
2. What do you see happening on which you have a strong opinion?
3. What information does your target market most need?

Capability Posts

Here are some questions to inspire this type of post:

1. What pain are people suffering from in your market and how could they find a solution?
2. What do people typically misunderstand or do wrong?
3. Which Playbook or tips might you share?

This should help to get started posting content and building your network.

To get your posts in front of more of the right people, it is essential to proactively build your network. Do this by sending out requests to connect, interacting and consistently commenting on people's content.

Your LinkedIn Scorecard

In terms of a scorecard, a productive week of online LinkedIn activity for job searching might be:

- Fifteen comments
- Fifty new connections
- Three content posts

I recommend you implement everything in this book, but if you only executed the material in one chapter, this is the most critical one.

Dive in and get started. Implement the strategies you've learned today, and you might like many others, be surprised by the results.

CHAPTER 8

Getting Fit For Interviews

Most people have an irrational fear of interviews and hate the idea of being assessed. From a powerful mindset perspective, it is vital to realise that interviews are very much a "two way" process. The interviewer is often more nervous than you!

I recommend you assess the employer as much as they assess you; after all, taking your next role is as big a decision for you as it is for them. When you approach interviews with this understanding, you will interview in a more effective way and enjoy more of a peer-to-peer style discussion rather than feeling as though you are being interrogated. People naturally perform better when they are calm because they think more clearly.

In the following two chapters I'm going to guide you through our interview playbook, and what to focus on and practise before, during and after the interview. I use the word "practise", deliberately, as the good news about interviewing is that like any skill you can improve it with practise. Before we get into techniques to ensure you perform at your best, let's explore the most common fatal interview flaws to avoid.

Fatal Interview Flaws

Having sat on hundreds of assessment panels and attended thousands of interviews, I've observed there are some common problems that stop good people from landing the roles they deserve.

Waffling

Nervous interviewees often feel compelled to fill the silence, which can cause them to talk too much and quickly turn to waffling. Waffling is fatal because you lose the interviewer and come across as someone who struggles with concise communication. When you catch yourself waffling, reign yourself in, take a breath and listen instead so you can decide what to say next.

Interview questions are not an invitation to air all of your knowledge or share the minutiae of your career. Give the interviewer concise and focused answers (more on this shortly) and round off your points succinctly. For interviews, remember that less is always more. If you've ever interviewed a candidate who didn't stop talking, you'll know it typically backfires and probably didn't create the impression they desired.

Interview Mode

Ah, the curse of the mind…overthinking. When we overthink in interviews, we are rarely present enough to provide an excellent account of ourselves. An interview is firstly a human-to-human interaction and the hiring decision will often be made on emotion before being justified by logic.

Let me reiterate. Interviewers decide emotionally and then justify their decision logically. And yet most performance interview research is based purely on fulfilling the technical or logical side of the interview. By the time the client shortlists five candidates for interview, it is likely that all the leaders who make the shortlist are well qualified to perform the role. It is therefore less likely to be a technical selection, but one based on who engages them the best and who the Line Manager would feel comfortable working with and introducing to key stakeholders.

On many occasions when I am interview-coaching with my clients, people who are usually engaging, warm and expressive, turn in to robots once the interview questions begin. The transformation is shocking and becomes like talking to a different person entirely.

If you fall in to "interview mode", then smile and remember to engage. Being present in the moment will always serve you better than regurgitating facts to impress the interviewer. Don't be an interview robot!

Being Over-keen

We mentioned this earlier in the book and need to revisit it again at this crucial point. It is not attractive for candidates to seem over-keen, particularly at the senior level, or they come across as desperate. When we researched this area in-depth, we found that the least keen candidates were more likely to be offered roles. Why? Well, winning candidates were more open, less defensive, more confident and able to build trust quicker. They were authentic, which is an attractive trait in a future colleague.

It comes down to human psychology—you're always more likely to receive something you don't show that you desperately need. Neediness is a turnoff; it repels. Interviews are a bit like dating! Even though you may feel you desperately need the job, remember that you are okay without it and a better one will come along if this one isn't meant to be. After all, you have nothing to lose because the job isn't yours. This doesn't mean you should take it to the extreme or you may come across as arrogant. Showing your natural enthusiasm is attractive, and it has a different energy to desperation. The interviewer will pick up on the subtle difference.

Lying

As we covered, interviewers decide emotionally and then back up their decision with logic. It takes a leap of faith to welcome a new leader into your tribe, and many hiring leaders go with their gut instinct. One thing you shouldn't do at an interview is lie. Typically, the interviewer will sense it, whether consciously or unconsciously, and you won't be hired. Many interviewees are tempted to fabricate and embellish their success, but I advise you never to do this. Be transparent to give yourself the best chance of being offered the role that suits you.

By being aware of these fatal floors, you can avoid them and will already be ahead of the competition during your next interview. Next, we'll dive into the power of research:

Research

Another way to get the edge is to prepare and research in a way which gives you the competitive advantage.

Whilst the current job market is more complex and nuanced than ever before, one of the key opportunities you have is to carry out research. Investing the time to go deep into every angle will give you all the insights and data you need to perform at your best on the day.

Here are the key research activities to prepare for your interview:

YouTube

This is my go-to channel and first port of call for interview research. Try to find videos of the interviewers in action because you will garner so much about their personal preferences and style. By the time you meet, you will already be familiar with the interviewer and know what to expect.

LinkedIn

Use this incredible platform to connect with people before you meet them, research their recommendations and read some of their posts so you get a feel for their personality.

Google News

This is a great way to see recent quotes, PR efforts, and industry news coverage of the company you are interviewing to join. You can easily set up Google alerts to keep you up-to-date. Arriving at the interview, informed of what the company is trying to achieve and the challenges they are facing, will help you stand out.

Website

This is the obvious place to spend some time. Pay particular attention to their vision, mission and values as the more yours align with theirs, the more likely they will resonate with you.

Print the Accounts

Gather as many available figures as possible to give you a feel for their financial performance and trends.

Agents on the Ground

Talk to any people you know who work there or who have previously worked there and see what you can learn about the behind-the-scenes leadership team and company culture.

Dress Code

This varies from company to company. Research dress code and present yourself accordingly on the day.

Learn their Language

Every business has a language which includes common turns of phrase and specific words that are important to them. Brush up on the terms they use at their website and in their materials and reflect on how to share this language naturally in your interview answers.

By taking the time to do this research, you will be better prepared than most other candidates. Armed with your research, you are now ready to rehearse your interview answers and hone your technique.

Rehearsal

The great news about interviews is that we can expect the common questions to come up and can rehearse appropriately. Whether you rehearse with a coach, a friend, or just record yourself and listen back, the benefits of interview practice are huge. Recording yourself on video is the best way because you'll not only pick up on areas to improve your delivery, but you will also notice weaknesses in body language and physical presentation. It can be disconcerting when you're not used to seeing yourself on video but stick with it because the momentary discomfort will dramatically propel you forward in the interview stakes.

As the military guys like to say: Proper preparation Prevents Piss Poor Performance—and interviews are no different.

Next, I'll share three of the most common questions you will encounter and how to ace them at interview.

1. **Please can you tell me about yourself and run me through your CV?**

Beware of the previously mentioned waffling trap. This question normally comes at the start of the interview as an icebreaker, and while you probably won't get hired based on your answer, you can get off to a poor start and lose the interviewer in an instant.

I have known candidates to talk for thirty minutes straight, going through every detail of their work history. To help people avoid this in our coaching at Executive Career Jump, we have what we call the 5/5/5 Framework for answering this question.

The aim is to answer in fewer than five minutes but to share five key career achievements and five key lessons along the way. This keeps it simple, concise and engaging and displays a powerful growth mindset.

Stick to this framework and you will do well. This is a great section to record and watch or listen back to, and make sure you deliver to the best of your ability. The interviewer has your detailed CV, so they don't need your complete life history. Give them the trailer, not the full movie!

2. What are your strengths and weaknesses?

Like many people, I dislike this question, but you can answer it successfully by following a simple rule: Give the interviewer a truthful strength which is vital for the role, and a truthful weakness that won't affect your success in the role.

It's pretty simple when you break it down and far better than the silly answers some people give to the weakness question such as being a "workaholic" or "over achiever". One pro-tip for the weakness question is to share the weakness (make sure it isn't related to a vital skill) and also explain how you are improving it. For example, for an IT Director role, you could say, "One weakness I have identified and worked on recently is public speaking. I have joined toast masters and watched various e-learning modules to try to further improve.".

This is open, honest, and shows an inclination for personal development and lifelong learning, rather than trying to manipulate the answer which can backfire and come across as arrogant.

3. Why do you want the role?

"Because I need a job" isn't an appropriate answer! Going back to their core values, practise an answer which will work for the interviewer both emotionally and logically. Make the answer meaningful and cover both the why and the what, and consider the following tips:

The Why

Why do the mission, vision, values, product or service mean something to you? Incorporate any personal experience in your answers.

The What

What you would bring to the role and what makes you a good fit for the Job Description requirements.

Reflecting on a combination of these two factors will ensure your answer stands out and positions you well.

I challenge you to have the goal of being the best prepared candidate in the interview shortlist in every process you enter. That way, whether or not you get the job, you will know you gave it your best shot and couldn't have done any more. You will also gain interview experience and nurture your confidence.

People frequently ask about the dangers of being over-rehearsed, and my answer is always the same: If you rehearse, it will help you to be fully present in the moment, knowing you are ready for the interview, and equipped to present your skills and character in the best light. When you prepare thoroughly, you will have more chance of talking naturally and being able to handle any unexpected questions. Trying to recite word-for-word scripts takes you away from being present in the moment, which is what people usually mean when they talk about being over-rehearsed.

Bring your best you to every interview and you'll have no regrets.

With this strong foundation in place, let's now jump ahead to the interview day and I'll share my top techniques and tips to help you attract more offers.

CHAPTER 9

Interview Performance

The day of your interview arrives, and if you've implemented the recommendations in the previous chapters, you couldn't be better prepared, and this represents an exciting opportunity for you.

It's important to nurture a calm mind to help you manage any interview nerves. Remember, interviewing is a two-way process; the interviewer has the challenge of finding a suitable candidate, and they may be as nervous as you.

If it appeals to you, I recommend leaders do a brief positive visualisation before their interview, where they imagine the meeting being a great success, and they genuinely like and enjoy a good connection with the interviewer.

Read positive reviews about the interviewer's management, study their content and in whatever way works for you, get yourself into a mental space where you are excited about meeting them. This is powerful because not only will your smile be authentic; your positivity will show on your face. Remember—a picture really is worth a thousand words. It's unusual not to warm to someone who clearly appreciates you, so you'll create a great first impression with the interviewer.

With the sudden rise in remote working, because of the COVID-19 Pandemic, and the available advanced video technology, video interviews have quickly become commonplace. People have been forced to embrace this rapid digital transformation whether or not they like it, and the workplace will never be the same.

Before we jump into techniques for the interview, let's cover tips for video interviews.

Test internet connection and technology

You are going to need about one megabyte per second in order to get a reliable video connection, so your internet connection doesn't let you down, interrupt your conversation or make you miss your interview altogether. I recommend you set up a call with the same software the interviewer uses and do a practice run with a friend or colleague. That way, any required software will be downloaded, you'll be familiar with how the programme works, and you'll know your internet coverage will meet your requirements. And if you don't have a smooth connection at home, you can organise an alternative location such as a quiet hotel lobby, which is a good solution for this type of scenario. If you find yourself in this situation, it's the perfect time to check out the best internet package for you to ensure a fast connection because besides video interviews, you could need a stable video connection for remote working. The interviewer may even ask whether this is an option for you.

Create a visual reminder to look at the camera

The more you talk to the camera rather than the person on the screen, the better you will deliver your answers and connect with the interviewer. Use a coloured dot on your laptop or some other visual reminder to make sure you look at the lens as it's easy to forget.

Optimum visibility

Position your laptop so you are at eye level, and if possible have natural light in front rather than framing you as that can make it difficult to see your face. This will ensure a clear picture and that your interviewer isn't blinded by the light, talking to your silhouette or looking up your nose!

Background and noise

I've heard horror stories of candidates forgetting to tidy their background. Some interviewed with laundry drying behind them, others had partially dressed family members walk by in the middle of an interview. While the interviewer will be interested in getting to know the 'real you', it is important to clean up your background, so you present yourself as a professional. Also, make sure other members of the house know you're on an important call and ask them to keep the noise down. Any type of distraction could throw you off, impact your performance, and ruin the first impression for your interviewer. There are virtual background options on many of the software applications, which can serve as a suitable alternative.

Use reminder notes

There are a couple of disadvantages to interviewing via video. It's more difficult to read body language and to judge the chemistry between you, than when meeting in person. But there is also one immense advantage: you can use reminder notes. You can stick reminder notes, prompts, and questions near your screen, and keep the key data in front of you. Make sure not to clutter up your space and don't let your notes distract you from responding authentically in the moment, as you don't want to come across as a rehearsed robot.

I recommend you turn up five minutes before the meeting start time. If you're earlier, you may be seen as too keen, and arriving late is of course a definite no-no. When interviewing in person, most candidates arrive early, grab a coffee nearby and read through their notes one more time as last-minute preparation.

Regardless of whether your interview is in person or via video, you will find the interview has a beginning, a middle and end, and next I will share tips that have helped many leaders perform at their best.

Beginning

First impressions count. If you are face to face, then focus on the basics which are: a firm handshake, confident smile, eye contact, good posture and body language. If you've prepared in the way we've covered, you will be ready to make the most of the interview.

Don't allow nerves to distract you from presenting yourself well. Even if you are nervous, one technique is to imagine you are playing the part of someone who isn't, or another is to give yourself permission to feel however you feel because nerves only dictate your performance if you focus on them. Learn to work with your nerves and recognise that feelings are a normal part of being human, and they simply mean that you care.

I recommend you begin the meeting with some rapport building and initial conversation: You can talk about the market, the business or any mutual acquaintances to help avoid awkwardness. As soon as you've established rapport, ask my No.1 gold-standard interview question.

Many executives I've coached have credited this question as the game-changer.

Ask permission:

Thanks again for inviting me in today. Just before we kick off, could I ask a question to help me get further context about what you're looking for?

Here is this simple yet powerful question:

If you were to fast-forward twelve months, what would have happened for you to feel like this hire had been an overwhelming success?

It's a brilliant question on several levels.

For a start, it gets the interviewer thinking, and showcases you as an outcome orientated candidate. But most importantly, it allows you to get under the skin of the requirements and to access what we call the "real job description".

Once you have this context, you can tailor your responses to their questions to ensure they meet their criteria.

Middle

In the middle portion of the interview, you're likely to face competency-based questions, which have become popular over the last decade because of the assumption that what happened in the past is an accurate prediction of the future. While this is a flawed idea because the future is unlikely to repeat the past, there are various mnemonics and acronyms used by candidates to help them navigate the questions and stay on track with their answers.

The most common is STAR:

The Star technique stands for Situation, Task, Action and Result. At Executive Career Jump, we add an E at the beginning which stands for Ethos, and a Q at the end which stands for Question. This creates: **ESTARQ**

When you answer competency questions, always answer in the first person with *I*, rather than *We* so that you own your answers and show you take responsibility for what happened and sell the journey as you share relevant case studies. As I said earlier, people make hiring decisions emotionally and justify them with logic. Interviewers want to hear about the journey: about your struggles and to understand the human element of what you achieved.

Let's begin with the Ethos

This is about how to communicate your ethos or motto regarding a particular topic. If the interviewer asks you about leadership, you weave your answer around your ethos, for example: "My approach to leadership is to offer freedom within a framework."

It's an overall ethos or motto, which sets you up for success regardless of the situation. And what is helpful about focusing on your ethos is that it gives you a framework you can easily remember and use in any situation in the future.

Once you've explained your ethos, go through the Situation, Task, Action, and Result of the case study.

If the interviewer asks you to give an example of when you've had to deal with a difficult customer, you would use the framework to plan your answer to reflect your case study like this:

My ethos of dealing with difficult customers is to have two ears and one mouth. I always seek to understand first and then to resolve the problem, and a good example of where this has come into my working life was when I worked with a major client in my previous role. The situation was that we hadn't delivered what we needed to deliver on time, and this caused the customer problems. My aim was to rebuild trust with the customer, and to resolve the immediate problem of getting the goods and services delivered.

I took several actions. The first was to look at the data and work out what had gone wrong. I identified a problem in the computer systems, which led to the lack of delivery. I took responsibility to communicate continuously with the customer to the point where they felt we were being transparent and keeping them in the loop every step of the way. The result was that we resolved the issue within twenty-four hours and gave them a discount on their next order to compensate for the inconvenience.

And within twelve months, they became our biggest account and championed us to other clients.

The Q is to remind us to finish our competency answers with a question.

Good examples are: "Did I cover everything you needed there?" or "Would you like any more detail on any element of that example?" or "How do you go about solving similar challenges internally?".

Adding a question to the end of your answers does two things:

1. It helps keep your answers shorter; rather than sharing every detail, you instead give the interviewer the option to find out more about the elements that are most important for them.
2. It keeps the conversation flowing.

Before every interview, go through the job description, and work out the different examples you're going to use for the necessary competencies and prepare those stories using the framework to keep you on track. Keep your answers focused so they show your competencies in the Action sections.

A classic question I've mentioned before but that is critical to flag again because it trips up so many interviewees is: "What are your strengths and weaknesses?"

People hate this question and get nervous, but I have a simple rule for you to use as part of your preparation and research which will stop you falling foul of this hard question. And the simple rule is, when asked, what your strengths and weaknesses are, be honest and pick an actual strength, which is vital for the role, and an actual weakness that isn't vital for the role.

Where people go wrong on this question is, they share a weakness that is disingenuous. They'll frequently claim a weakness that they think the interviewer will see as a strength, such as "I'm a workaholic," or "I don't suffer fools gladly," or "I'm a perfectionist."

Answers of this nature come over as manipulative and will typically backfire, positioning you as someone with an ego who secretly thinks they don't have any weaknesses.

End

Finally, it's important to wrap up the interview successfully.

Remember that people reflect on the questions you ask almost as much as the answers you give. The interviewer will typically ask whether you have questions, and I recommend you have several insightful ones ready.

Here are three questions I share with my clients:

1. How do the company values play out internally?
2. What is the right mix of people and technology in the business?
3. How do you think I would fit with the team?

The last question is a smart way to find out if they've got any concerns and gives you the chance to address any objections face-to-face.

Follow Up

Follow up with an email on the same day. Thank the interviewer for their time, reconfirm your interest in the role (if you still want it), and offer references to back up your case studies and confirm what you said in the meeting.

In the next chapter we'll cover how to ace those critical presentations.

CHAPTER 10

Final Stage Presentations

If you fully executed our Interview Playbook, there's a high chance you will quickly find yourself in the latter stages of an assessment process. Whether the role has emerged from the hidden job market or from a job advert, the final hurdles typically involve a presentation or a case study element, so the interviewer sees you in action to help them decide whether you can deliver on your promises.

Feeling nervous about delivering an important presentation is natural. Channel that energy positively to motivate you to do the necessary preparation, so that you are ready to perform at your best. Remember, you are the same person who was successful in the past, so if your pesky inner critic shows up, don't take their words seriously! You can also revisit the mindset chapter to help shift you into the optimum mental space should you feel a little shaky. The good news is I also have an excellent Presentations Playbook to share with you, which is a major factor in my company helping many leaders secure their desired job offers.

Before we get into that, I want to highlight the importance of receiving feedback throughout your job searching activities. Genuine feedback following a performance at an interview is a rare gift if you can get it. Always be willing and open to receive feedback, rather than defensive or argumentative, which is so often the default setting when people feel insecure. We learn nothing new to help us improve if we're not open to genuine feedback.

Interviewees find employers play it safe by giving them pointless generic statements as feedback, such as, 'You were great, but you were just pipped to the post.' Or, 'Other applicants were slightly better suited.' Or that old classic, 'You didn't have the right experience.' These empty declarations are useless, but this type of feedback allows the interviewers to get off lightly without having to risk an uncomfortable conversation, and candidates are afraid of hearing anything negative, so they don't push for more. I call this: *the happy ears phenomenon.*

Rather than protecting your feelings, I recommend you proceed to the last stage of an interview, by asking for feedback from the hiring team or recruiter representing you before the final meeting. They may not share everything openly, but if they offer some insights, you'll be going to the last stage fully armed with information you need to address the hiring team's concerns and have your best shot at securing the role.

Remember, it's perfectly normal for them to have some concerns. In my experience, there are always concerns during the assessment as senior hires carry a lot of risk. Whether they have some doubts about your skills and worry you're too experienced, not experienced enough, lack drive or even that you are too ambitious, the chances are they'll have some reservations. What you need to do is focus on the specific doubt that's playing on their minds, so you can address it in the meeting.

The other occasion when you'll have an opportunity for feedback is when you're rejected following an interview. I know you'll probably be feeling a little bruised, but this is the perfect time to use the experience to improve for your next interview. I discovered a more powerful way of extracting insights rather than asking for feedback in the traditional way which I'll share with you now:

Go back to anybody who decided not to proceed with your application and ask them to share the three things you could work on before your next interview.

This is powerful because it forces the hiring leader to give you valuable takeaways that you can act on. Make this a habit and part of your job search process and remember not to be defensive, even if you don't agree with what they say.

After the feedback and before the last stage, is when they're most likely to ask you to present or go through some kind of case study activity.

Let's now review the typical assessment formats so you know what to expect.

Final stage presentations fall into three formats:

The first is the 90-day plan, the second is a go-to-market plan, and the third is a personal presentation about why you're the right candidate for the role.

All three formats have their merits, but whichever they ask you to deliver, these are the key goals:

In the 90-day plan, people are looking to establish your priorities and methodologies. For a go-to-market plan, people are looking to establish your commercial acumen, how well aligned your thought process is with theirs, and where you see the opportunities. In the why you're the right candidate, people are looking to assess your ability to tell stories.

The good news is that there are more software options available for you to use for your presentations than ever before. If you wish to put a presentation together in advance, check out Prezi, or even basic PowerPoint themes will do the job to ensure your slides are attractive and present your key messages.

Throughout this book, I've guided you through how to avoid fatal flaws on various topics, and now we'll look at how to avoid common fatal flaws when delivering presentations.

Fatal Flaws

1. Handing out printed slide booklets

This is an extremely common error. People print out their sides and when they enter the room to present, they hand everyone in the room a copy of the slides before they present. The problem with this common practice is many of the people in the room read ahead and pay more attention to the printed slides instead of engaging with your live presentation. You also reduce the impact of your presentation as there will be no surprises. For most presentations, I recommend not handing out slides in advance.

2. Death by PowerPoint

We've all sat through presentations which have droned on for too long and have been painful to absorb. A common problem with PowerPoint is people cram in too much text on each slide and then read the text from the slides. This is a dull, low-impact way to present because the audience quickly loses interest as they scan ahead. Consider what they need you for if they can get all the information from the slides! Instead, lead the presentation in a relaxed way so the audience connects with you and hangs on your every word.

3. Not meeting the brief or being too generic

Candidates are frequently tempted to present what they wish to present rather than what the brief asks them to present. It's critical to tailor your presentation to the brief they gave you, so you show your ability to correctly interpret information and deliver exactly what they want.

4. Running over time

If they allocate you fifteen minutes for a presentation, make the presentation slightly shorter; maximum fourteen minutes so you don't run over trying to wrap up. You won't gain any points by trying to deliver a forty-five-minute presentation in a fifteen-minute time slot. You'll either try to say too much, run over and annoy attendees, or run out of time and not complete your presentation. Any of these undesirable outcomes will reduce your chances of a job offer and show a general lack of ability to follow instructions.

5. Video

Many interviews now take place over the internet, but there are certain things that don't work as well on video interviews as they do in person. A good example is sharing videos in your presentation, whether via Zoom, Teams or any other platform, technology can be challenging and temperamental. My recommendation, if you are presenting online, is not to embed any video into your slides and instead keep the format as simple as possible.

By being aware of these fatal flaws, you can prepare and set yourself up for success.

Another important thing to think about is what the assessors are specifically looking for. What insights are they after during interviews?

Here are my thoughts on the key things they're looking to assess:

1. Your knowledge

They want to learn what ideas you have, what you know and how you can translate your experience to get them to a better future.

2. How you deliver

They want to examine the detail of what you will deliver; not only your recommendations, but how you would go about executing them. A challenge for many leaders is they excel at strategy but are not as accomplished in execution. I have found that a lot of assessors look for evidence of successful execution.

3. Observations

They frequently wish to assess your observations, and so the more you include your observations in your presentation, the better because it shows an ability to extract data from situations. It also shows an ability to listen and means you'll be adding value before you formally begin work.

4. Culture fit

They'll be evaluating whether you appear to be someone they want to work with; whom they can imagine collaborating around the table and fitting in with their environment, difficult stakeholders and other partners. Keep this in mind when you prepare and deliver your presentation.

Structuring your presentation for success is obviously a critical piece of the puzzle, and an excellent model to follow is the legendary Guy Kawasaki's 10/20/30 rule:

The presentation should last for only ten minutes, have no more than twenty slides and use no smaller than size thirty font. This is a simple framework I have used repeatedly that has set me and my clients up for success.

I also recommend you make sure your presentations flow. At Executive Career Jump, we have a particular Framework we apply to all case studies and presentations: We always produce slides that cover the Why, What, How, Who, Case study and the Summary.

Let's go through each section because if you prepare for all of them, you'll be ready for most presentation scenarios:

Why

The goal is to set the scene, so focus on the big picture and the macro trends that inform the recommendations you will make. The format would typically be one of stats and bullets, and I recommend you dial them into the company vision, relevant trends and insights.

What

The goal is to convey credibility and instil confidence that you know what you're doing. The format for this will be about sharing observations and goals, but also a concept: some kind of vision you're aiming for and what your model will be because showing a model makes it more of a reality for your audience. I've seen people use alliterative models such as Three Cs or Mnemonics. It must be something simple that distils your plan into an easy-to-understand slide.

How

The goal is to make sure that you're seen as *the* person to implement this change. It goes back to showing your ability to execute the strategy you propose. Good formats include a grid, a scorecard, or a timeline.

Who

The goal is to cover the people elements which many presenters skip.

This piece is about the people you will take on the journey with you and how you're going to handle the people element of delivering your strategy.

Case Study

The goal is to present a highly relevant example, so choose your Case Study with care. I recommend you include a slide which shows how you've successfully executed your recommendations in the past.

Summary

The goal is to bring everything together in one slide and refer back to the task and your key messages.

The summary is about relevance to the original brief and how your Why, What, How, Who and Case Study deliver against that brief.

Prepare for a Q&A session with the questions likely to come up and have some well-rehearsed answers for if they question you on details of your presentation.

Put your presentation aside for a while and then come back with fresh eyes to review it thoroughly. It's a good idea to ask a trusted contact to pick it apart and ask questions that come up. This additional preparation will make sure you expect and are prepared to answer all questions to the best of your ability.

By implementing everything in this chapter, it is likely you will receive job offers soon. Next, we'll cover the important topic of salary negotiations.

CHAPTER 11

Offer Management and Salary Negotiation

We've covered everything you need to create successful presentations so in this chapter we'll move into how to manage those job offers!

Let's begin with the most common error leaders make at this point:

Making It A Battle

There will be plenty of opportunities for you and your new boss to show off your commercial and negotiation prowess when you work together. However, during salary negotiations, make sure you keep that ego in check! If you make it a competition, then someone will inevitably enter the new working relationship feeling like they lost, which is not the way to establish trust. Instead, be open and aim to work together on the solution, rather than in competition, so the outcome is a win-win.

I recommend you don't come across as greedy, as it will put you under severe pressure to deliver quickly rather than effectively.

Negotiation is about finding levers you can pull to create the package that feels like a good mix of risk and reward for both parties.

And now let's look at my top tips for successful negotiations:

Tip 1. Let the Headhunter Help

When I was a Headhunter, many candidates tried to negotiate directly and leave us out of the loop, which is an error. A headhunter can play a vital role as a broker and ensure that you don't suffer any of the potential damage caused to the relationship as described above. Headhunters are typically paid a percentage of your base salary, which means you are aligned financially, and they will have your best interests at heart.

Tip 2. Focus on the Size of the Prize

In the Interview chapter we spoke about the magic question that every leader should ask at the start of an interview: "Fast forward twelve months, what would have to happen for you to feel like this has been an overwhelming success?". Besides helping you uncover the real job description, the answer to this question is also helpful in negotiating your salary, particularly if you can get the hiring team to a put a number on what success would look like. For example: They want to grow by three million or improve profit by two million.

By referring to their goal as part of your negotiation strategy, you can position your salary as an investment rather than a cost. You tie your salary to the numerical pay-off you aim to help deliver and that way your value is clearly showcased. Think about it…when the prize is an additional two million, that extra ten thousand you ask for doesn't seem like such a big ask.

Tip 3. Use Direct Approaches

As described in our go-to-market strategy, headhunters are an excellent channel for job searching. But when you apply for a job directly or are approached, there is one big advantage for salary negotiations, which is there is no fee attached to your introduction.

With the average recruitment fee at around twenty percent, that is a sizeable chunk of cash associated with your hire that will not be incurred if there is no headhunter or other agency involved. At negotiation time, this frees up a bigger margin to play with and can allow extra compensation for you while not going over budget.

Tip 4. Use Evidence

The assumption when people negotiate is that they over inflate previous earnings, so showing statements or contracts with proof of income is a simple way to be transparent and prove you are being fair with your salary request.

Tip 5. Focus on the At-Risk Components

Experience has shown me that companies are more likely to be flexible on the At-Risk components of the package, rather than on the base salary. With that in mind, if you can't get the higher salary offer you want, focus on increasing the bonus potential based on results so that if you deliver the desired outcome, your compensation reflects the results and makes up any shortfall on the base salary.

These tips are designed to help you extract more value from your job offers. But what if you receive multiple offers?

Deciding Between Offers

This can be tricky, but as in the adage about London buses, I often find people who work with us at Executive Career Jump (even those who have been on the job market for a while) receive more than one job offer at the same time, once they implement our strategies.

This relates to what we covered in the Mindset chapter in this book, and the idea of attracting, not chasing. Once people receive one offer, they typically relax, answer questions more honestly and become a more attractive prospect so it's like a virtuous circle. Candidates are less attractive when they're uptight and desperate, but when they relax and feel more confident, job offers typically roll in.

Let's say you have more than one job offer, and the decision feels overwhelming. You don't want to make a wrong step, let anyone down or find yourself back on the market again soon.

For this critical piece of securing your ideal job, I devised an effective weighted scorecard which shows you how to remove the emotion and guesswork from your decision.

Scorecard—The Five Ps

Test each job offer against what I call the Five Ps, which are: **Product, Progression, Package, Purpose and Person**.

Mark your interest in the **Product**, out of ten.

How passionate are you about the company's services and products?

Next, take each role you've been offered and mark them all on **Progression**, out of fifteen.

How much stretch is in the role and future progression opportunities? When people feel they are progressing, they are more likely to be motivated.

Then mark the **Package**, out of twenty.

The best way to do this is to mark each offer out of ten, using the base salary and then out of ten on the total compensation and benefits which together give you a score out of twenty.

The fourth P is **Purpose** and should be marked out of twenty-five.

How much purpose we find in our work is vital in terms of fulfilment, and there have been many studies done on the benefits of combining who we are with what we do.

Mark each role and consider how much each one aligns with your values.

The fifth and final P is for **Person** and we mark this out of thirty, so it carries a higher weight than the others.

This is about the person you will work for. I've found that more than any other element, this is the most accurate predictor of fulfilment. What does your gut say about how well you resonate with this person?

Add up the results and you will have a score out of one hundred for each role, which is balanced and weighted in a way that makes it easier for you to make the right choice.

I've got one final but important tip for this chapter regarding counter offers. Don't accept them!

If you resign from your post, but then receive a counteroffer in a desperate effort to keep you on, my strong recommendation is to not accept it. There may be the odd occasion where it makes sense, but typically it doesn't. You decided to leave for a valid reason, and retrospective rewards and attention rarely work out well in the long term. There are stats available about this which show many people who backtrack and accept a counteroffer, leave the post within six months, and have to go through the process of leaving all over again.

As referenced throughout this book, the modern world of job searching is nuanced and most senior roles are in what I call "The hidden job market".

To help you execute all we have covered in this book, so you can effectively tap into this hidden market, the next chapter contains a summary of key takeaways and action points.

Whether you've already taken the steps as you worked through the book, or whether you read the whole book first and are about to begin, the following summary will help ensure you've covered everything to get you on the fast track to receiving your ideal job offers.

10 Step Action Plan

To help you execute on the advice in this book here is a simple 10 step plan you can follow to put this playbook into action:

Step 1. Type up your own mission statement (Chapter 4)
Step 2. Create a Job search Activity Tracker (Chapter 5)
Step 3. Download our ATS CV template and create your own (Chapter 5)
Step 4. Update and Optimise your LinkedIn Profile (Chapter 7)
Step 5. Send out a note to your KPIs offering your time (Chapter 6)
Step 6. Post a "Flare Post" on LinkedIn to alert your network (Chapter 7)
Step 7. Create a LinkedIn scorecard and start posting to your audience (Chapter 7)
Step 8. Create an interview cheat sheet with your answers to the most common questions (Chapter 8)
Step 9. Practice and refine telling your CV story (Chapter 8)
Step 10. Block out time in your diary for the next four weeks based on the Job Search Playbook. (Chapter 5)

BONUS CHAPTER

The First Ninety Days

Let's say you have landed your new role. Congratulations—great work! In this Bonus Chapter, we'll look at how to avoid common pitfalls, and make your first ninety days a huge success.

The first ninety days in a new leadership role can be tricky. Typically, you'll be trying to balance a range of emotions when you're in a probation period and aware that people are making early judgements and analysing who you are and what you are about.

The most common challenge with the first ninety days is the race to deliver a return on the investment of hiring you and proving you can walk your talk. No one likes to feel they're an overhead, and no one wants to think they made a poor hiring choice. You may also be frustrated as the newbie on the team who has to learn a new business language and internalise a range of new colleague relationships and products all at once. It's not unusual to feel overwhelmed; even anxious, but you can channel these feelings as a positive driving force when you know how to harness their power.

Navigating the Ninety Day Dip

One thing to be wary of is what I call the "Ninety Day Dip" which refers to the fact that when you join a new business, your motivation will be at an all-time high.

You will start the new role full of hope and optimism and excited by the feeling of a clean slate and fresh challenge. The trouble is that while for a fleeting moment, this incredible feeling is wonderfully energising, your motivation is liable to decline when the initial euphoria wears off. The trajectory of the decline usually depends on the quality of the onboarding you receive, combined with the way you think and act, which directly relates to your understanding of how motivation works.

This **Ninety Day Dip** is a well-documented phenomenon where around the ninety-day mark, people often begin feeling stressed about the future and grasp the size of the challenge for which they signed up. This is that pivotal moment you may recognise from past endeavours when you've taken on a new challenge—suddenly everything seems deadly serious and the challenge looks like Everest! Your perspective changes and things look difficult or even impossible and you doubt your abilities. You may even have trouble remembering why you were so enthused and confident at the beginning!

Most people go through some type of dip; especially when they don't understand how their mind plays tricks on them, and they take those pesky insecure thoughts seriously. It also happens when people get promoted into a new role. They pushed hard to get the promotion and fell under the illusion that achieving what they wanted would magically fix everything, but then they woke up to the cold reality that the job was tougher than they expected and brought with it all the usual problems and challenges. This is the human condition!

Humans—especially High Achievers, fall foul of the popular misunderstanding that by achieving their goals, they will somehow be permanently satisfied, but what usually happens is they get a temporary high, and then quickly move on to the next thing they decide they must achieve to be fulfilled. Then life becomes a tiresome cycle of, 'If only this happens, or I can have "this" (whatever "this" may be), I will be happy then.' It may sound simplistic but think about it because it is how most people unconsciously operate, and it's the only thing standing between you feeling more of that initial good euphoric feeling, more of the time.

This is one reason I developed the scorecard. When you select the role most suited to your values and aspirations, rather than taking the role you think you SHOULD want, as the initial euphoria wears off—which I guarantee it will—you are more likely to stay engaged and enjoy your new challenge.

While everybody experiences some kind of ninety-day adjustment, the name of the game is to help you navigate any dip gracefully, which is easier to do when you understand why it's happening, and that it is only a fearful state of mind. When you know this simple yet little-known truth, you don't have to take your state of mind seriously and can move through it quickly when a new thought pops into your head. Thoughts cannot hurt you; remember they are an illusion!

How to Navigate the Ninety Day Dip

You can avoid the classic archetypes that result in catastrophic ninety-day problems by being aware of them:

Archetypes

The Bull in the China Shop

Pent up with the anxiety of proving their worth and having an impact, the Bull in the China Shop charges in to the ninety-day period and creates havoc. It is as if every person, process and product is bright red, and they must smash them up and rebuild them, to show how great they are. This is a fast way to destroy trust, alienate the people on your team, and create chaos.

Captain Hindsight

This is the leader who joins and tells everyone what should have happened before they turned up! We've all met people who behave like this. It's annoying, comes across as smug, and while doing a "black box" challenge type of exercise may be constructive after negative events have occurred, this type of approach doesn't build connection or trust, and just irritates the people who've been working hard before you arrived.

The Procrastinator

They spend their time analysing, undertaking diagnostics and planning but they miss one critical thing: action! The Procrastinator is the antithesis of the Bull in the China Shop in that by ensuring they don't "throw the baby out with the bath water" they don't make any progress at all. As with any progress, done is better than perfect and sometimes you have to make some moves to gather the data you need to decide what you next step is.

The Rebounder

I came up with this term for those who obsess about the ex, which in this context is the former employer—not a reference to romantic relationships. The Rebounder talks about their old employer constantly, shares endless anecdotes about their old team and clients, and spends much of their time looking in the rear-view mirror, rather than being present and looking through the windscreen at the road ahead. It's difficult to form productive new relationships when you are obsessed with old ones.

Some of those Archetypes may have resonated with you based on your experience of seeing new leaders in action. Avoid them and you'll be off to a solid start.

There are three rules of engagement we use in my company for the first ninety days to help guide people to early success as they navigate the dip:

Rule No.1. Two ears, one mouth

Listen more than you speak. Listen to customers, stakeholders, and to your new team. The practice of "Active Listening", not only helps build trust but also gives you vital insights to inform your strategy on what happens next.

Rule No.2. Find the quick wins

A sensible balance between the Procrastinator and the Bull in the China Shop is to take considered action, but also secure some quick early wins. Finding low hanging fruit that you pick off easily and help deliver results and value straight away, is a simple way to eliminate the risk element for you and your new employer.

Rule No.3. Have a no-surprises policy

When you join a business, the speed with which you are effective is often directly correlated to your ability to build trust. The essential relationships to get right are those with your new boss and team. From the start of your tenure, make sure that bad news travels as fast as good news and over-communicate both upwards and downwards so that there are no surprises. Throughout my career, I have never met a team that complained that their new boss over-communicated with them!

Sticking with this approach should help you assimilate fast and begin building the next stage of your career positively. You may also want to work with a mentor or coach during the first ninety days as many executives find this gives them the edge, and they have a sounding board to test out their ideas.

When you join an organisation, you have a brief window of time when you naturally view the business with "fresh eyes", before you integrate into the culture and the fabric. Don't let it slip by without maximising the opportunity.

The roles are out there, and people need your help. Your first job is to find them, which should be a lot simpler now you know what to do.

I would like to thank you for buying and reading this book, and I wish you incredible success in your job search and next opportunity.

Printed in Great Britain
by Amazon